DAILY DEVOTIONAL JOURNAL
PRAYER, INSPIRATIONS AND GRATITUDE

Devotional Journal

If Found Return To

Name

Address

Phone

Email

Company Name

Address

Phone

Email

As a Reward: $

Sunday

DATE: _____

TODAY I WILL MAKE AN EFFORT TO WORSHIP THE LORD BY

THE BIBLE VERSE ON MY HEART RIGHT NOW: _____

Three things i am praying for this week

1. _____
2. _____
3. _____

THIS IS THE BIBLICAL TRUTH I AM GOING TO HOLD ONTO GOING IN TO THIS WEEK
(SERMON NOTE, A BIBLE VERSE, DEVOTIONAL QUOTE, ETC)

_____
_____
_____
_____

PEOPLE IN MY LIFE THAT I CAN BE PRAYING FOR RIGHT NOW

NAME : .... NAME : .... NAME : .... NAME : ....

Prayer: Prayer: Prayer: Prayer:

Monday

DATE:_____

HOW DO I FEEL TODAY?_____

RIGHT NOW, I AM LOOKING FORWARD TO

I will make the most of today by doing this

- -

- -

- -

THE MOST MEMORABLE PART OF THIS WEEKEND WAS ...

THE BIBLE VERSE I WILL CLING TO TODAY IS

MY MORNING PRAYER

Tuesday

DATE: _____

Today will be different from yesterday because

- -

- -

- -

TODAY I WILL BE PRAYING FOR

HOW I WILL MAKE AN EFFORT TO BE MORE LIKE JESUS TODAY

THIS IS THE BIBLE VERSE I WILL REMEMBER TODAY WHEN MY TO-DO LIST AS I WORK MY WAY THROUGH MY DAILY ROUTINE (WRITE IT OUT BELOW)

I AM THANKFUL FOR

Wednesday

DATE: _____

Things To Do Today

- -

- -

- -

A SONG THAT REMINDS ME NOT TO STRESS:

THE VERSE AND MY PRAYER I WILL LEAN INTO TODAY IS

- -

- -

- -

- -

- -

- -

SOMETHING I WILL DO TO RELAX TODAY, EVEN IF IT'S JUST FOR A FEW MINUTES:

Thursday

DATE:_____

This is what God has shown me in my life this week so far

TODAY I WILL CHALLENGE MY SELF TO:

- -
- -
- -

Here are 3 people I am thinking of today or will interact with today and here's how I will pray for them.

NAME :................................   NAME :................................   NAME :................................

Prayer: **Prayer:**   **Prayer:**

THE BIBLE VERSE THAT STANDS OUT TO ME THE MOST TODAY IS...

- -
- -
- -

Friday

DATE:_____

THE FIRST THING I WILL THANK GOD FOR TODAY IS

- -

The very first thing I thought about this morning was

- -

The most exciting thing about today will be

- -

After I'm finished with my responsibilities today I planning on

MY FRIDAY MORNING PRAYER

- -

- -

- -

- -

- -

The part of this week that stood out to me the most was

_____

_____

_____

_____

NOTES

_____

_____

_____

Saturday

DATE:_____

MY PRAYER FOR TODAY

. . . .

. . . .

. . . .

. . . .

Here are a few things God did in my life this week

- -

- -

- -

- -

Here's what i have planned for the day

_____

_____

_____

Here's the name of a person i can make an effort to encourage today

Today is different than last Saturday because:_____

_____

_____

Sunday

DATE: _____

TODAY I WILL MAKE AN EFFORT TO WORSHIP THE LORD BY

THE BIBLE VERSE ON MY HEART RIGHT NOW: _____

Three things i am praying for this week

1. _____
2. _____
3. _____

THIS IS THE BIBLICAL TRUTH I AM GOING TO HOLD ONTO GOING IN TO THIS WEEK
(SERMON NOTE, A BIBLE VERSE, DEVOTIONAL QUOTE, ETC)

_____
_____
_____
_____

PEOPLE IN MY LIFE THAT I CAN BE PRAYING FOR RIGHT NOW

NAME : ....   NAME : ....   NAME : ....   NAME : ....

Prayer: Prayer: Prayer: Prayer:

Monday

DATE:_____

HOW DO I FEEL TODAY?_____

RIGHT NOW, I AM LOOKING FORWARD TO

I will make the most of today by doing this

- -
- -
- -

THE MOST MEMORABLE PART OF THIS WEEKEND WAS ...

THE BIBLE VERSE I WILL CLING TO TODAY IS

MY MORNING PRAYER

Tuesday

DATE:_____

Today will be different from yesterday because

- -

- -

- -

TODAY I WILL BE PRAYING FOR

HOW I WILL MAKE AN EFFORT TO BE MORE LIKE JESUS TODAY

THIS IS THE BIBLE VERSE I WILL REMEMBER TODAY WHEN MY TO-DO LIST AS I WORK MY WAY THROUGH MY DAILY ROUTINE (WRITE IT OUT BELOW)

I AM THANKFUL FOR

Wednesday

DATE: _____

Things To Do Today

- -
- -
- -

A SONG THAT REMINDS ME NOT TO STRESS:

THE VERSE AND MY PRAYER I WILL LEAN INTO TODAY IS

- -
- -
- -
- -
- -

SOMETHING I WILL DO TO RELAX TODAY, EVEN IF IT'S JUST FOR A FEW MINUTES:

Thursday

DATE: _____

This is what God has shown me in my life this week so far

TODAY I WILL CHALLENGE MY SELF TO:

- -

- -

- -

Here are 3 people I am thinking of today or will interact with today and here's how I will pray for them.

NAME : _____ NAME : _____ NAME : _____

Prayer: Prayer: Prayer:

THE BIBLE VERSE THAT STANDS OUT TO ME THE MOST TODAY IS...

- -

- -

- -

Friday

DATE:_____

THE FIRST THING I WILL THANK GOD FOR TODAY IS

- -

The very first thing I thought about this morning was

- -

The most exciting thing about today will be

- -

After I'm finished with my responsibilities today I planning on

MY FRIDAY MORNING PRAYER

- -

- -

- -

- -

The part of this week that stood out to me the most was

_____

_____

_____

_____

NOTES

_____

_____

_____

Saturday

DATE: _____

MY PRAYER FOR TODAY

. . . .

. . . .

. . . .

. . . .

Here are a few things God did in my life this week

- -

- -

- -

- -

Here's what i have planned for the day

_____

_____

_____

Here's the name of a person i can make an effort to encourage today

Today is different than last Saturday because: _____

_____

_____

Sunday

DATE: _____

TODAY I WILL MAKE AN EFFORT TO WORSHIP THE LORD BY

THE BIBLE VERSE ON MY HEART RIGHT NOW: _____

Three things i am praying for this week

1. _____
2. _____
3. _____

THIS IS THE BIBLICAL TRUTH I AM GOING TO HOLD ONTO GOING IN TO THIS WEEK
(SERMON NOTE, A BIBLE VERSE, DEVOTIONAL QUOTE, ETC)

_____

_____

_____

_____

PEOPLE IN MY LIFE THAT I CAN BE PRAYING FOR RIGHT NOW

NAME :_____ NAME :_____ NAME :_____ NAME :_____

Prayer: Prayer: Prayer: Prayer:

Monday

DATE:_____

HOW DO I FEEL TODAY?_____

RIGHT NOW, I AM LOOKING FORWARD TO

I will make the most of today by doing this

- -
- -
- -

THE MOST MEMORABLE PART OF THIS WEEKEND WAS ...

THE BIBLE VERSE I WILL CLING TO TODAY IS

MY MORNING PRAYER

Tuesday

DATE: _____

Today will be different from yesterday because

- -

- -

- -

TODAY I WILL BE PRAYING FOR

HOW I WILL MAKE AN EFFORT TO BE MORE LIKE JESUS TODAY

THIS IS THE BIBLE VERSE I WILL REMEMBER TODAY WHEN MY TO-DO LIST AS I WORK MY WAY THROUGH MY DAILY ROUTINE (WRITE IT OUT BELOW)

I AM THANKFUL FOR

Wednesday

DATE:_____

Things To Do Today

A SONG THAT REMINDS ME NOT TO STRESS:

THE VERSE AND MY PRAYER I WILL LEAN INTO TODAY IS

SOMETHING I WILL DO TO RELAX TODAY, EVEN IF IT'S JUST FOR A FEW MINUTES:

Thursday

DATE: _____

This is what God has shown me in my life this week so far

TODAY I WILL CHALLENGE MY SELF TO:

- -

- -

- -

Here are 3 people I am thinking of today or will interact with today and here's how I will pray for them.

NAME :_____   NAME :_____   NAME :_____

Prayer: Prayer: Prayer:

THE BIBLE VERSE THAT STANDS OUT TO ME THE MOST TODAY IS...

- -

- -

- -

Friday

DATE:_____

THE FIRST THING I WILL THANK GOD FOR TODAY IS

- -

The very first thing I thought about this morning was

- -

The most exciting thing about today will be

- -

After I'm finished with my responsibilities today I planning on

MY FRIDAY MORNING PRAYER

- -
- -
- -
- -
- -

The part of this week that stood out to me the most was

_____

_____

_____

_____

NOTES

_____

_____

_____

Saturday

DATE:_____

MY PRAYER FOR TODAY

. . . .

. . . .

. . . .

. . . .

Here are a few things God did in my life this week

- -

- -

- -

- -

Here's what i have planned for the day

_____

_____

_____

Here's the name of a person i can make an effort to encourage today

Today is different than last Saturday because: _____

_____

_____

Sunday

DATE:_____

TODAY I WILL MAKE AN EFFORT TO WORSHIP THE LORD BY

THE BIBLE VERSE ON MY HEART RIGHT NOW: _____

Three things i am praying for this week

1. _____
2. _____
3. _____

THIS IS THE BIBLICAL TRUTH I AM GOING TO HOLD ONTO GOING IN TO THIS WEEK
(SERMON NOTE, A BIBLE VERSE, DEVOTIONAL QUOTE, ETC)

_____

_____

_____

_____

PEOPLE IN MY LIFE THAT I CAN BE PRAYING FOR RIGHT NOW

NAME :....................   NAME :....................   NAME :....................   NAME :....................

Prayer: Prayer: Prayer: Prayer:

Monday

DATE:_____

HOW DO I FEEL TODAY?_____

RIGHT NOW, I AM LOOKING FORWARD TO

I will make the most of today by doing this

- -
- -
- -

THE MOST MEMORABLE PART OF THIS WEEKEND WAS ...

THE BIBLE VERSE I WILL CLING TO TODAY IS

MY MORNING PRAYER

Tuesday

DATE:_____

Today will be different from yesterday because

TODAY I WILL BE PRAYING FOR

HOW I WILL MAKE AN EFFORT TO BE MORE LIKE JESUS TODAY

THIS IS THE BIBLE VERSE I WILL REMEMBER TODAY WHEN MY TO-DO LIST AS I WORK MY WAY THROUGH MY DAILY ROUTINE (WRITE IT OUT BELOW)

I AM THANKFUL FOR

Wednesday

DATE:_____

Things To Do Today

- -
- -
- -

A SONG THAT REMINDS ME NOT TO STRESS:

THE VERSE AND MY PRAYER I WILL LEAN INTO TODAY IS

- -
- -
- -
- -
- -
- -

SOMETHING I WILL DO TO RELAX TODAY, EVEN IF IT'S JUST FOR A FEW MINUTES:

Thursday

DATE: _____

This is what God has shown me in my life this week so far

TODAY I WILL CHALLENGE MY SELF TO:

- -

- -

- -

Here are 3 people I am thinking of today or will interact with today and here's how I will pray for them.

NAME :.................................

NAME :.................................

NAME :.................................

Prayer:

Prayer:

Prayer:

THE BIBLE VERSE THAT STANDS OUT TO ME THE MOST TODAY IS...

- -

- -

- -

Friday

DATE:_____

THE FIRST THING I WILL THANK GOD FOR TODAY IS

- -

The very first thing I thought about this morning was

- -

The most exciting thing about today will be

- -

After I'm finished with my responsibilities today I planning on

MY FRIDAY MORNING PRAYER

- -

- -

- -

- -

The part of this week that stood out to me the most was

_____

_____

_____

_____

NOTES

_____

_____

_____

Saturday

DATE:_____

MY PRAYER FOR TODAY

. . . .

. . . .

. . . .

. . . .

Here are a few things God did in my life this week

- -

- -

- -

- -

Here's what i have planned for the day

_____

_____

_____

Here's the name of a person i can make an effort to encourage today

Today is different than last Saturday because: _____

_____

_____

Sunday

DATE: _____

TODAY I WILL MAKE AN EFFORT TO WORSHIP THE LORD BY

[   ]

THE BIBLE VERSE ON MY HEART RIGHT NOW: _____

Three things i am praying for this week

1. _____
2. _____
3. _____

THIS IS THE BIBLICAL TRUTH I AM GOING TO HOLD ONTO GOING IN TO THIS WEEK
(SERMON NOTE, A BIBLE VERSE, DEVOTIONAL QUOTE, ETC)

_____
_____
_____
_____

PEOPLE IN MY LIFE THAT I CAN BE PRAYING FOR RIGHT NOW

NAME : _____   NAME : _____   NAME : _____   NAME : _____

Prayer: Prayer: Prayer: Prayer:

Monday

DATE:_____

HOW DO I FEEL TODAY?_____

RIGHT NOW, I AM LOOKING FORWARD TO

I will make the most of today by doing this

- -

- -

- -

THE MOST MEMORABLE PART OF THIS WEEKEND WAS ...

THE BIBLE VERSE I WILL CLING TO TODAY IS

MY MORNING PRAYER

Tuesday

DATE: _____

Today will be different from yesterday because

TODAY I WILL BE PRAYING FOR

HOW I WILL MAKE AN EFFORT TO BE MORE LIKE JESUS TODAY

THIS IS THE BIBLE VERSE I WILL REMEMBER TODAY WHEN MY TO-DO LIST AS I WORK MY WAY THROUGH MY DAILY ROUTINE (WRITE IT OUT BELOW)

I AM THANKFUL FOR

Wednesday

DATE:_____

Things To Do Today

- -
- -
- -

A SONG THAT REMINDS ME NOT TO STRESS:

THE VERSE AND MY PRAYER I WILL LEAN INTO TODAY IS

- -
- -
- -
- -
- -

SOMETHING I WILL DO TO RELAX TODAY, EVEN IF IT'S JUST FOR A FEW MINUTES:

Thursday

DATE:_____

This is what God has shown me in my life this week so far

TODAY I WILL CHALLENGE MY SELF TO:

Here are 3 people I am thinking of today or will interact with today and here's how I will pray for them.

NAME :............................ NAME :............................ NAME :............................

Prayer: **Prayer:**   **Prayer:**

THE BIBLE VERSE THAT STANDS OUT TO ME THE MOST TODAY IS...

Friday

DATE:_____

THE FIRST THING I WILL THANK GOD FOR TODAY IS

- -

The very first thing I thought about this morning was

- -

The most exciting thing about today will be

- -

After I'm finished with my responsibilities today I planning on

MY FRIDAY MORNING PRAYER

- -

- -

- -

- -

- -

The part of this week that stood out to me the most was

_____

_____

_____

_____

NOTES

_____

_____

Saturday

DATE:_____

MY PRAYER FOR TODAY

. . . .

. . . .

. . . .

. . . .

Here are a few things God did in my life this week

- -

- -

- -

- -

Here's what i have planned for the day

_____

_____

_____

Here's the name of a person i can make an effort to encourage today

Today is different than last Saturday because: _____

_____

_____

Sunday

DATE: _____

TODAY I WILL MAKE AN EFFORT TO WORSHIP THE LORD BY

THE BIBLE VERSE ON MY HEART RIGHT NOW: _____

Three things i am praying for this week

1. _____
2. _____
3. _____

THIS IS THE BIBLICAL TRUTH I AM GOING TO HOLD ONTO GOING IN TO THIS WEEK
(SERMON NOTE, A BIBLE VERSE, DEVOTIONAL QUOTE, ETC)

PEOPLE IN MY LIFE THAT I CAN BE PRAYING FOR RIGHT NOW

NAME : _____ NAME : _____ NAME : _____ NAME : _____

Prayer: Prayer: Prayer: Prayer:

Monday

DATE: _____

HOW DO I FEEL TODAY? _____

RIGHT NOW, I AM LOOKING FORWARD TO

I will make the most of today by doing this

- -
- -
- -

THE MOST MEMORABLE PART OF THIS WEEKEND WAS ...

THE BIBLE VERSE I WILL CLING TO TODAY IS

MY MORNING PRAYER

Tuesday

DATE:_____

Today will be different from yesterday because

- -

- -

- -

TODAY I WILL BE PRAYING FOR

HOW I WILL MAKE AN EFFORT TO BE MORE LIKE JESUS TODAY

THIS IS THE BIBLE VERSE I WILL REMEMBER TODAY WHEN MY TO-DO LIST
AS I WORK MY WAY THROUGH MY DAILY ROUTINE (WRITE IT OUT BELOW)

I AM THANKFUL FOR

Wednesday

DATE: _____

Things To Do Today

- -
- -
- -

A SONG THAT REMINDS ME NOT TO STRESS:

THE VERSE AND MY PRAYER I WILL LEAN INTO TODAY IS

- -
- -
- -
- -
- -

SOMETHING I WILL DO TO RELAX TODAY, EVEN IF IT'S JUST FOR A FEW MINUTES:

Thursday

DATE: _____

This is what God has shown me in my life this week so far

TODAY I WILL CHALLENGE MY SELF TO:

Here are 3 people I am thinking of today or will interact with today and here's how I will pray for them.

NAME :.................................   NAME :.................................   NAME :.................................

Prayer: Prayer: Prayer:

THE BIBLE VERSE THAT STANDS OUT TO ME THE MOST TODAY IS...

Friday

DATE:_____

THE FIRST THING I WILL THANK GOD FOR TODAY IS

- -

THE VERY FIRST THING I THOUGHT ABOUT THIS MORNING WAS

- -

THE MOST EXCITING THING ABOUT TODAY WILL BE

- -

After I'm finished with my responsibilities today I planning on

MY FRIDAY MORNING PRAYER

- -

- -

- -

- -

- -

The part of this week that stood out to me the most was

_____

_____

_____

_____

NOTES

_____

_____

_____

Saturday

DATE:_____

MY PRAYER FOR TODAY

. . . .

. . . .

. . . .

. . . .

Here are a few things God did in my life this week

- -

- -

- -

- -

Here's what i have planned for the day

_____

_____

_____

Here's the name of a person i can make an effort to encourage today

Today is different than last Saturday because: _____

_____

_____

Sunday

DATE:_____

TODAY I WILL MAKE AN EFFORT TO WORSHIP THE LORD BY

THE BIBLE VERSE ON MY HEART RIGHT NOW: _____

Three things i am praying for this week

1. _____
2. _____
3. _____

THIS IS THE BIBLICAL TRUTH I AM GOING TO HOLD ONTO GOING IN TO THIS WEEK
(SERMON NOTE, A BIBLE VERSE, DEVOTIONAL QUOTE, ETC)

_____
_____
_____
_____

PEOPLE IN MY LIFE THAT I CAN BE PRAYING FOR RIGHT NOW

NAME :_____ NAME :_____ NAME :_____ NAME :_____

Prayer: Prayer: Prayer: Prayer:

Monday

DATE:_____

HOW DO I FEEL TODAY?_____

RIGHT NOW, I AM LOOKING FORWARD TO

I will make the most of today by doing this

- -

- -

- -

THE MOST MEMORABLE PART OF THIS WEEKEND WAS ...

THE BIBLE VERSE I WILL CLING TO TODAY IS

MY MORNING PRAYER

Tuesday

DATE: _____

Today will be different from yesterday because

- -

- -

- -

TODAY I WILL BE PRAYING FOR

HOW I WILL MAKE AN EFFORT TO BE MORE LIKE JESUS TODAY

THIS IS THE BIBLE VERSE I WILL REMEMBER TODAY WHEN MY TO-DO LIST
AS I WORK MY WAY THROUGH MY DAILY ROUTINE (WRITE IT OUT BELOW)

I AM THANKFUL FOR

Wednesday

DATE:_____

Things To Do Today

- -

- -

- -

A SONG THAT REMINDS ME NOT TO STRESS:

THE VERSE AND MY PRAYER I WILL LEAN INTO TODAY IS

- -

- -

- -

- -

- -

SOMETHING I WILL DO TO RELAX TODAY, EVEN IF IT'S JUST FOR A FEW MINUTES:

Thursday

DATE: _____

This is what God has shown me in my life this week so far

TODLY I WILL CHALLENGE MY SELF TO:

- -
- -
- -

Here are 3 people I am thinking of today or will interact with today and here's how I will pray for them.

NAME :_____   NAME :_____   NAME :_____

Prayer: Prayer: Prayer:

THE BIBLE VERSE THAT STANDS OUT TO ME THE MOST TODAY IS...

- -
- -
- -

Friday

DATE:_____

THE FIRST THING I WILL THANK GOD FOR TODAY IS

- -

The very first thing I thought about this morning was

- -

The most exciting thing about today will be

- -

After I'm finished with my responsibilities today I planning on

MY FRIDAY MORNING PRAYER

- -

- -

- -

- -

- -

The part of this week that stood out to me the most was

_____

_____

_____

_____

NOTES

_____

_____

_____

Saturday

DATE:_____

MY PRAYER FOR TODAY

. . . .

. . . .

. . . .

. . . .

Here are a few things God did in my life this week

- -

- -

- -

Here's what i have planned for the day

_____

_____

_____

Here's the name of a person i can make an effort to encourage today

Today is different than last Saturday because: _____

_____

_____

Sunday

DATE: _____

TODAY I WILL MAKE AN EFFORT TO WORSHIP THE LORD BY

[ ]

THE BIBLE VERSE ON MY HEART RIGHT NOW: _____

Three things i am praying for this week

1. _____
2. _____
3. _____

THIS IS THE BIBLICAL TRUTH I AM GOING TO HOLD ONTO GOING IN TO THIS WEEK
(SERMON NOTE, A BIBLE VERSE, DEVOTIONAL QUOTE, ETC)

_____
_____
_____

PEOPLE IN MY LIFE THAT I CAN BE PRAYING FOR RIGHT NOW

NAME : ....   NAME : ....   NAME : ....   NAME : ....

Prayer: Prayer: Prayer: Prayer:

Monday

DATE:_____

HOW DO I FEEL TODAY?_____

RIGHT NOW, I AM LOOKING FORWARD TO

I will make the most of today by doing this

- -
- -
- -

THE MOST MEMORABLE PART OF THIS WEEKEND WAS ...

THE BIBLE VERSE I WILL CLING TO TODAY IS

MY MORNING PRAYER

Tuesday

DATE: _____

Today will be different from yesterday because

- -

- -

- -

TODAY I WILL BE PRAYING FOR

HOW I WILL MAKE AN EFFORT TO BE MORE LIKE JESUS TODAY

THIS IS THE BIBLE VERSE I WILL REMEMBER TODAY WHEN MY TO-DO LIST AS I WORK MY WAY THROUGH MY DAILY ROUTINE (WRITE IT OUT BELOW)

I AM THANKFUL FOR

Wednesday

DATE: _____

Things To Do Today

- -

- -

- -

A SONG THAT REMINDS ME NOT TO STRESS:

THE VERSE AND MY PRAYER I WILL LEAN INTO TODAY IS

- -

- -

- -

- -

- -

SOMETHING I WILL DO TO RELAX TODAY, EVEN IF IT'S JUST FOR A FEW MINUTES:

Thursday

DATE:_____

This is what God has shown me in my life this week so far

TODAY I WILL CHALLENGE MY SELF TO:

- -

- -

- -

Here are 3 people I am thinking of today or will interact with today and here's how I will pray for them.

NAME :........................ NAME :........................ NAME :........................

Prayer: Prayer: Prayer:

THE BIBLE VERSE THAT STANDS OUT TO ME THE MOST TODAY IS...

- -

- -

- -

Friday

DATE: _____

THE FIRST THING I WILL THANK GOD FOR TODAY IS

- -

The very first thing I thought about this morning was

- -

The most exciting thing about today will be

- -

After I'm finished with my responsibilities today I planning on

MY FRIDAY MORNING PRAYER

- -

- -

- -

- -

The part of this week that stood out to me the most was

_____

_____

_____

_____

NOTES

_____

_____

_____

Saturday

DATE: _____

MY PRAYER FOR TODAY

· ·

· ·

· ·

· ·

Here are a few things God did in my life this week

- -

- -

- -

- -

Here's what i have planned for the day

_____

_____

_____

Here's the name of a person i can make an effort to encourage today

Today is different than last Saturday because: _____

_____

_____

Sunday

DATE:_____

TODAY I WILL MAKE AN EFFORT TO WORSHIP THE LORD BY

THE BIBLE VERSE ON MY HEART RIGHT NOW: _____

Three things i am praying for this week

1. _____
2. _____
3. _____

THIS IS THE BIBLICAL TRUTH I AM GOING TO HOLD ONTO GOING IN TO THIS WEEK
(SERMON NOTE, A BIBLE VERSE, DEVOTIONAL QUOTE, ETC)

_____
_____
_____
_____

PEOPLE IN MY LIFE THAT I CAN BE PRAYING FOR RIGHT NOW

NAME :_____ NAME :_____ NAME :_____ NAME :_____

Prayer: Prayer: Prayer: Prayer:

Monday

DATE:_____

HOW DO I FEEL TODAY?_____

RIGHT NOW, I AM LOOKING FORWARD TO

I will make the most of today by doing this

- -
- -
- -

THE MOST MEMORABLE PART OF THIS WEEKEND WAS ...

THE BIBLE VERSE I WILL CLING TO TODAY IS

MY MORNING PRAYER

Tuesday

DATE: _____

Today will be different from yesterday because

TODAY I WILL BE PRAYING FOR

HOW I WILL MAKE AN EFFORT TO BE MORE LIKE JESUS TODAY

THIS IS THE BIBLE VERSE I WILL REMEMBER TODAY WHEN MY TO-DO LIST AS I WORK MY WAY THROUGH MY DAILY ROUTINE (WRITE IT OUT BELOW)

I AM THANKFUL FOR

Wednesday

DATE: _____

Things To Do Today

- -

- -

- -

A SONG THAT REMINDS ME NOT TO STRESS:

THE VERSE AND MY PRAYER I WILL LEAN INTO TODAY IS

- -

- -

- -

- -

- -

- -

SOMETHING I WILL DO TO RELAX TODAY, EVEN IF IT'S JUST FOR A FEW MINUTES:

Thursday

DATE:_____

This is what God has shown me in my life this week so far

TODAY I WILL CHALLENGE MY SELF TO:

- -
- -
- -

Here are 3 people I am thinking of today or will interact with today and here's how I will pray for them.

NAME :_____   NAME :_____   NAME :_____

Prayer: Prayer: Prayer:

THE BIBLE VERSE THAT STANDS OUT TO ME THE MOST TODAY IS...

- -
- -

Friday

DATE:_____

THE FIRST THING I WILL THANK GOD FOR TODAY IS

- -

The very first thing I thought about this morning was

- -

The most exciting thing about today will be

- -

After I'm finished with my responsibilities today I planning on

MY FRIDAY MORNING PRAYER

- -

- -

- -

- -

- -

The part of this week that stood out to me the most was

_____

_____

_____

_____

NOTES

_____

_____

_____

Saturday

DATE:_____

MY PRAYER FOR TODAY

. . . .

. . . .

. . . .

. . . .

Here are a few things God did in my life this week

- -

- -

- -

- -

Here's what i have planned for the day

_____

_____

_____

Here's the name of a person i can make an effort to encourage today

Today is different than last Saturday because: _____

_____

_____

Sunday

DATE:_____

TODAY I WILL MAKE AN EFFORT TO WORSHIP THE LORD BY

THE BIBLE VERSE ON MY HEART RIGHT NOW: _____

Three things i am praying for this week

1. _____
2. _____
3. _____

THIS IS THE BIBLICAL TRUTH I AM GOING TO HOLD ONTO GOING IN TO THIS WEEK
(SERMON NOTE, A BIBLE VERSE, DEVOTIONAL QUOTE, ETC)

_____
_____
_____

PEOPLE IN MY LIFE THAT I CAN BE PRAYING FOR RIGHT NOW

NAME :.................   NAME :.................   NAME :.................   NAME :.................

Prayer: Prayer: Prayer: Prayer:

Monday

DATE:_____

HOW DO I FEEL TODAY?_____

RIGHT NOW, I AM LOOKING FORWARD TO

I will make the most of today by doing this

THE MOST MEMORABLE PART OF THIS WEEKEND WAS ...

THE BIBLE VERSE I WILL CLING TO TODAY IS

MY MORNING PRAYER

Tuesday

DATE:_____

Today will be different from yesterday because

- -

- -

- -

TODAY I WILL BE PRAYING FOR

HOW I WILL MAKE AN EFFORT TO BE MORE LIKE JESUS TODAY

THIS IS THE BIBLE VERSE I WILL REMEMBER TODAY WHEN MY TO-DO LIST
AS I WORK MY WAY THROUGH MY DAILY ROUTINE (WRITE IT OUT BELOW)

I AM THANKFUL FOR

Wednesday

DATE: _____

Things To Do Today

- -
- -
- -

A SONG THAT REMINDS ME NOT TO STRESS:

THE VERSE AND MY PRAYER I WILL LEAN INTO TODAY IS

- -
- -
- -
- -
- -
- -

SOMETHING I WILL DO TO RELAX TODAY, EVEN IF IT'S JUST FOR A FEW MINUTES:

Thursday

DATE:_____

This is what God has shown me in my life this week so far

TODAY I WILL CHALLENGE MY SELF TO:

- -

- -

- -

Here are 3 people I am thinking of today or will interact with today and here's how I will pray for them.

NAME :.............................. NAME :.............................. NAME :..............................

Prayer: Prayer: Prayer:

THE BIBLE VERSE THAT STANDS OUT TO ME THE MOST TODAY IS...

- -

- -

- -

Friday

DATE:_____

THE FIRST THING I WILL THANK GOD FOR TODAY IS

- -

The very first thing I thought about this morning was

- -

The most exciting thing about today will be

- -

After I'm finished with my responsibilities today I planning on

MY FRIDAY MORNING PRAYER

- -

- -

- -

- -

The part of this week that stood out to me the most was

_____

_____

_____

_____

NOTES

_____

_____

_____

Saturday

DATE:_____

MY PRAYER FOR TODAY

· ·

· ·

· ·

· ·

Here are a few things God did in my life this week

- -

- -

- -

- -

Here's what i have planned for the day

_____

_____

_____

Here's the name of a person i can make an effort to encourage today

Today is different than last Saturday because: _____

_____

_____

Sunday

DATE:_____

TODAY I WILL MAKE AN EFFORT TO WORSHIP THE LORD BY

THE BIBLE VERSE ON MY HEART RIGHT NOW: _____

Three things i am praying for this week

1. _____
2. _____
3. _____

THIS IS THE BIBLICAL TRUTH I AM GOING TO HOLD ONTO GOING IN TO THIS WEEK
(SERMON NOTE, A BIBLE VERSE, DEVOTIONAL QUOTE, ETC)

_____
_____
_____
_____

PEOPLE IN MY LIFE THAT I CAN BE PRAYING FOR RIGHT NOW

NAME :_____ NAME :_____ NAME :_____ NAME :_____

Prayer: Prayer: Prayer: Prayer:

Monday

DATE:_____

HOW DO I FEEL TODAY?_____

RIGHT NOW, I AM LOOKING FORWARD TO

I will make the most of today by doing this

- -

- -

- -

THE MOST MEMORABLE PART OF THIS WEEKEND WAS ...

THE BIBLE VERSE I WILL CLING TO TODAY IS

MY MORNING PRAYER

Tuesday

DATE: _____

Today will be different from yesterday because

- -

- -

- -

TODAY I WILL BE PRAYING FOR

HOW I WILL MAKE AN EFFORT TO BE MORE LIKE JESUS TODAY

THIS IS THE BIBLE VERSE I WILL REMEMBER TODAY WHEN MY TO-DO LIST
AS I WORK MY WAY THROUGH MY DAILY ROUTINE (WRITE IT OUT BELOW)

I AM THANKFUL FOR

Wednesday

DATE: _____

Things To Do Today

- -
- -
- -

A SONG THAT REMINDS ME NOT TO STRESS:

THE VERSE AND MY PRAYER I WILL LEAN INTO TODAY IS

- -
- -
- -
- -
- -

SOMETHING I WILL DO TO RELAX TODAY, EVEN IF IT'S JUST FOR A FEW MINUTES:

Thursday

DATE:_____

This is what God has shown me in my life this week so far

TODAY I WILL CHALLENGE MY SELF TO:

- -

- -

- -

Here are 3 people I am thinking of today or will interact with today and here's how I will pray for them.

NAME :_____   NAME :_____   NAME :_____

Prayer: Prayer: Prayer:

THE BIBLE VERSE THAT STANDS OUT TO ME THE MOST TODAY IS...

- -

- -

- -

Friday

DATE:_____

THE FIRST THING I WILL THANK GOD FOR TODAY IS

- -

The very first thing I thought about this morning was

- -

The most exciting thing about today will be

- -

After I'm finished with my responsibilities today I planning on

MY FRIDAY MORNING PRAYER

- -

- -

- -

- -

- -

The part of this week that stood out to me the most was

_____

_____

_____

_____

NOTES

_____

_____

_____

Saturday

DATE:_____

MY PRAYER FOR TODAY

. . . .

. . . .

. . . .

. . . .

Here are a few things God did in my life this week

- -

- -

- -

- -

Here's what i have planned for the day

_____

_____

_____

Here's the name of a person i can make an effort to encourage today

Today is different than last Saturday because: _____

_____

_____

Sunday

DATE:_____

TODAY I WILL MAKE AN EFFORT TO WORSHIP THE LORD BY

THE BIBLE VERSE ON MY HEART RIGHT NOW: _____

Three things i am praying for this week

1. _____
2. _____
3. _____

THIS IS THE BIBLICAL TRUTH I AM GOING TO HOLD ONTO GOING IN TO THIS WEEK
(SERMON NOTE, A BIBLE VERSE, DEVOTIONAL QUOTE, ETC)

_____
_____
_____
_____

PEOPLE IN MY LIFE THAT I CAN BE PRAYING FOR RIGHT NOW

NAME :........................   NAME :........................   NAME :........................   NAME :........................

Prayer: Prayer: Prayer: Prayer:

Monday

DATE:_____

HOW DO I FEEL TODAY?_____

RIGHT NOW, I AM LOOKING FORWARD TO

I will make the most of today by doing this

- -
- -
- -

THE MOST MEMORABLE PART OF THIS WEEKEND WAS ...

THE BIBLE VERSE I WILL CLING TO TODAY IS

MY MORNING PRAYER

Tuesday

DATE:_____

Today will be different from yesterday because

- -

- -

- -

TODAY I WILL BE PRAYING FOR

HOW I WILL MAKE AN EFFORT TO BE MORE LIKE JESUS TODAY

THIS IS THE BIBLE VERSE I WILL REMEMBER TODAY WHEN MY TO-DO LIST AS I WORK MY WAY THROUGH MY DAILY ROUTINE (WRITE IT OUT BELOW)

I AM THANKFUL FOR

Wednesday

DATE:_____

Things To Do Today

A SONG THAT REMINDS ME NOT TO STRESS:

THE VERSE AND MY PRAYER I WILL LEAN INTO TODAY IS

SOMETHING I WILL DO TO RELAX TODAY, EVEN IF IT'S JUST FOR A FEW MINUTES:

Thursday

DATE: _____

This is what God has shown me in my life this week so far

TODO I WILL CHALLENGE MY SELF TO:

Here are 3 people I am thinking of today or will interact with today and here's how I will pray for them.

NAME :_____   NAME :_____   NAME :_____

Prayer: Prayer: Prayer:

THE BIBLE VERSE THAT STANDS OUT TO ME THE MOST TODAY IS...

Friday

DATE:_____

THE FIRST THING I WILL THANK GOD FOR TODAY IS

- -

The very first thing I thought about this morning was

- -

The most exciting thing about today will be

- -

After I'm finished with my responsibilities today I planning on

MY FRIDAY MORNING PRAYER

- -

- -

- -

- -

- -

The part of this week that stood out to me the most was

_____

_____

_____

_____

NOTES

_____

_____

_____

Saturday

DATE:_____

MY PRAYER FOR TODAY

· ·

· ·

· ·

· ·

Here are a few things God did in my life this week

- -

- -

- -

Here's what i have planned for the day

_____

_____

_____

Here's the name of a person i can make an effort to encourage today

Today is different than last Saturday because: _____

_____

_____

Sunday

DATE:_____

TODAY I WILL MAKE AN EFFORT TO WORSHIP THE LORD BY

THE BIBLE VERSE ON MY HEART RIGHT NOW: _____

Three things i am praying for this week

1. _____
2. _____
3. _____

THIS IS THE BIBLICAL TRUTH I AM GOING TO HOLD ONTO GOING IN TO THIS WEEK
(SERMON NOTE, A BIBLE VERSE, DEVOTIONAL QUOTE, ETC)

_____
_____
_____
_____

PEOPLE IN MY LIFE THAT I CAN BE PRAYING FOR RIGHT NOW

NAME :_____   NAME :_____   NAME :_____   NAME :_____

Prayer: Prayer: Prayer: Prayer:

Monday

DATE:_____

HOW DO I FEEL TODAY?_____

RIGHT NOW, I AM LOOKING FORWARD TO

I will make the most of today by doing this

- -
- -
- -

THE MOST MEMORABLE PART OF THIS WEEKEND WAS ...

THE BIBLE VERSE I WILL CLING TO TODAY IS

MY MORNING PRAYER

Tuesday

DATE:_____

Today will be different from yesterday because

- -

- -

- -

TODAY I WILL BE PRAYING FOR

HOW I WILL MAKE AN EFFORT TO BE MORE LIKE JESUS TODAY

THIS IS THE BIBLE VERSE I WILL REMEMBER TODAY WHEN MY TO-DO LIST AS I WORK MY WAY THROUGH MY DAILY ROUTINE (WRITE IT OUT BELOW)

I AM THANKFUL FOR

Wednesday

DATE:_____

Things To Do Today

- -

- -

- -

A SONG THAT REMINDS ME NOT TO STRESS:

THE VERSE AND MY PRAYER I WILL LEAN INTO TODAY IS

- -

- -

- -

- -

- -

SOMETHING I WILL DO TO RELAX TODAY, EVEN IF IT'S JUST FOR A FEW MINUTES:

Thursday

DATE:_____

This is what God has shown me in my life this week so far

TODAY I WILL CHALLENGE MY SELF TO:

- -
- -
- -

Here are 3 people I am thinking of today or will interact with today and here's how I will pray for them.

NAME :_____   NAME :_____   NAME :_____

Prayer: Prayer: Prayer:

THE BIBLE VERSE THAT STANDS OUT TO ME THE MOST TODAY IS...

- -
- -

Friday

DATE:_____

THE FIRST THING I WILL THANK GOD FOR TODAY IS

- -

The very first thing I thought about this morning was

- -

The most exciting thing about today will be

- -

After I'm finished with my responsibilities today I planning on

MY FRIDAY MORNING PRAYER

- -

- -

- -

- -

The part of this week that stood out to me the most was

_____

_____

_____

_____

NOTES

_____

_____

_____

Saturday

DATE:_____

MY PRAYER FOR TODAY

....

....

....

....

Here are a few things God did in my life this week

- -

- -

- -

- -

Here's what i have planned for the day

_____

_____

_____

Here's the name of a person i can make an effort to encourage today

Today is different than last Saturday because: _____

_____

_____

Sunday

DATE: _____

TODAY I WILL MAKE AN EFFORT TO WORSHIP THE LORD BY

[ ]

THE BIBLE VERSE ON MY HEART RIGHT NOW: _____

Three things i am praying for this week

1. _____
2. _____
3. _____

THIS IS THE BIBLICAL TRUTH I AM GOING TO HOLD ONTO GOING IN TO THIS WEEK
(SERMON NOTE, A BIBLE VERSE, DEVOTIONAL QUOTE, ETC)

_____
_____
_____
_____

PEOPLE IN MY LIFE THAT I CAN BE PRAYING FOR RIGHT NOW

NAME : ....   NAME : ....   NAME : ....   NAME : ....

Prayer: Prayer: Prayer: Prayer:

Monday

DATE:_____

HOW DO I FEEL TODAY?_____

RIGHT NOW, I AM LOOKING FORWARD TO

I will make the most of today by doing this

- -
- -
- -

THE MOST MEMORABLE PART OF THIS WEEKEND WAS ...

THE BIBLE VERSE I WILL CLING TO TODAY IS

MY MORNING PRAYER

Tuesday

DATE:_____

Today will be different from yesterday because

TODAY I WILL BE PRAYING FOR

HOW I WILL MAKE AN EFFORT TO BE MORE LIKE JESUS TODAY

THIS IS THE BIBLE VERSE I WILL REMEMBER TODAY WHEN MY TO-DO LIST AS I WORK MY WAY THROUGH MY DAILY ROUTINE (WRITE IT OUT BELOW)

I AM THANKFUL FOR

Wednesday

DATE: _____

Things To Do Today

- -
- -
- -

A SONG THAT REMINDS ME NOT TO STRESS:

THE VERSE AND MY PRAYER I WILL LEAN INTO TODAY IS

- -
- -
- -
- -
- -

SOMETHING I WILL DO TO RELAX TODAY, EVEN IF IT'S JUST FOR A FEW MINUTES:

Thursday

DATE: _____

This is what God has shown me in my life this week so far

TODAY I WILL CHALLENGE MY SELF TO:

- -

- -

- -

Here are 3 people I am thinking of today or will interact with today and here's how I will pray for them.

NAME :.. NAME :................................... .... NAME :....................................

Prayer:

Prayer:

Prayer:

THE BIBLE VERSE THAT STANDS OUT TO ME THE MOST TODAY IS...

- -

- -

- -

Friday

DATE:_____

THE FIRST THING I WILL THANK GOD FOR TODAY IS

- -

The very first thing I thought about this morning was

- -

The most exciting thing about today will be

- -

After I'm finished with my responsibilities today I planning on

MY FRIDAY MORNING PRAYER

- -

- -

- -

- -

The part of this week that stood out to me the most was

_____

_____

_____

_____

NOTES

_____

_____

_____

Saturday

DATE:_____

MY PRAYER FOR TODAY

. . . .

. . . .

. . . .

. . . .

Here are a few things God did in my life this week

- -

- -

- -

- -

Here's what i have planned for the day

_____

_____

_____

Here's the name of a person i can make an effort to encourage today

Today is different than last Saturday because: _____

_____

_____

Sunday

DATE:_____

TODAY I WILL MAKE AN EFFORT TO WORSHIP THE LORD BY

THE BIBLE VERSE ON MY HEART RIGHT NOW: _____

Three things i am praying for this week

1. _____
2. _____
3. _____

THIS IS THE BIBLICAL TRUTH I AM GOING TO HOLD ONTO GOING IN TO THIS WEEK
(SERMON NOTE, A BIBLE VERSE, DEVOTIONAL QUOTE, ETC)

PEOPLE IN MY LIFE THAT I CAN BE PRAYING FOR RIGHT NOW

NAME :_____ NAME :_____ NAME :_____ NAME :_____

Prayer: Prayer: Prayer: Prayer:

Monday

DATE:_____

HOW DO I FEEL TODAY?_____

RIGHT NOW, I AM LOOKING FORWARD TO

I will make the most of today by doing this

- -

- -

- -

THE MOST MEMORABLE PART OF THIS WEEKEND WAS ...

THE BIBLE VERSE I WILL CLING TO TODAY IS

MY MORNING PRAYER

Tuesday

DATE: _____

Today will be different from yesterday because

- -

- -

- -

TODAY I WILL BE PRAYING FOR

HOW I WILL MAKE AN EFFORT TO BE MORE LIKE JESUS TODAY

THIS IS THE BIBLE VERSE I WILL REMEMBER TODAY WHEN MY TO-DO LIST
AS I WORK MY WAY THROUGH MY DAILY ROUTINE (WRITE IT OUT BELOW)

I AM THANKFUL FOR

Wednesday

DATE: _____

Things To Do Today

A SONG THAT REMINDS ME NOT TO STRESS:

THE VERSE AND MY PRAYER I WILL LEAN INTO TODAY IS

SOMETHING I WILL DO TO RELAX TODAY, EVEN IF IT'S JUST FOR A FEW MINUTES:

Thursday

DATE: _____

This is what God has shown me in my life this week so far

TODAY I WILL CHALLENGE MY SELF TO:

Here are 3 people I am thinking of today or will interact with today and here's how I will pray for them.

NAME : _____ NAME : _____ NAME : _____

Prayer:

Prayer:

Prayer:

THE BIBLE VERSE THAT STANDS OUT TO ME THE MOST TODAY IS...

Friday

DATE:_____

THE FIRST THING I WILL THANK GOD FOR TODAY IS

- -

The very first thing I thought about this morning was

- -

The most exciting thing about today will be

- -

After I'm finished with my responsibilities today I planning on

MY FRIDAY MORNING PRAYER

- -

- -

- -

- -

- -

The part of this week that stood out to me the most was

_____

_____

_____

_____

NOTES

_____

_____

_____

Saturday

DATE:_____

MY PRAYER FOR TODAY

. . . .

. . . .

. . . .

. . . .

Here are a few things God did in my life this week

- -

- -

- -

- -

Here's what i have planned for the day

_____

_____

_____

Here's the name of a person i can make an effort to encourage today

Today is different than last Saturday because: _____

_____

_____

Made in the USA
Coppell, TX
18 June 2020